THE BLUEBELL RAILWAY REVISITED

MATT ALLEN

HALSGROVE

First published in Great Britain in 2013

Copyright © Matt Allen 2013

British Library Cataloguing-in-Publication Data
A CIP record for this title is available from the British Library

ISBN 978 0 85704 209 5

HALSGROVE
Halsgrove House,
Ryelands Business Park,
Bagley Road, Wellington, Somerset TA21 9PZ
Tel: 01823 653777 Fax: 01823 216796
email: sales@halsgrove.com
website: www.halsgrove.com

Printed and bound in China by Everbest Printing Co Ltd

INTRODUCTION

The *Bluebell Railway Revisited* enables the Halsgrove Railway Series to return to the Bluebell Railway following on from the original book released back in 2008. The railway has experienced a number of developments in recent years, in particular achieving the huge milestone of completing the extension to East Grinstead with the first trains running the entirety of the line from Sheffied Park to East Grinstead in March 2013. This is a significant achievement by what is, effectively, a mainly volunteer run railway. The £4 Million "Northern Extension" Project involved moving 75,000 tonnes of rubbish from the cutting at Imberhorne, which had been used as a refuse disposal site. Clearing the site and returning it to its former use is one of the biggest achievements in railway preservation. The extension from Kingscote to East Grinstead adds 2 miles to the original 9 mile line and now provides the railway with a much coveted mainline connection at East Grinstead. The mainline connection, restored 55 years after it was removed, allows trains to run from the mainline straight onto Bluebell metals. At East Grinstead a new station platform has been built a few hundred metres from the East Grinstead mainline station. This provides great opportunities for day trippers to travel down from London to East Grinstead on the mainline electric services and change to the Bluebell for a steam ride to Sheffield Park.

This book will take you on a trip along the line, where you will see the fantastic variety of superbly restored steam locomotives, rolling stock, visiting locomotives, authentic stations and of course the new section of line to East Grinstead.

The railway is one of the country's biggest tourist attractions with well over 180,000 visitors per year. It is also one of the major Heritage Railways in the UK providing a home for a great selection of mainly Southern rolling stock and locomotives. With the advent of the new mainline connection it will be interesting to see if the railway becomes a base for mainline certified steam locomotives for use on the national network. The mainline connectivity will certainly allow mainline specials to run direct onto the Bluebell Railway: imagine getting on a steam-hauled train at London Victoria and running through to Sheffield Park!

Looking back at its history, originally the Bluebell Railway was a part of the Lewes to East Grinstead Railway. The L&EGR (as it was known) was originally promoted in 1876, the chairman of the L&EGR being the Earl of Sheffield who owned Sheffield Park. However, the project didn't get off the ground until the L&EGR approached the London, Brighton and South Coast Railway for assistance in 1878. On 1 August 1882 the line from Lewes to East Grinstead was opened; the line was primarily intended for freight use with passengers being a secondary concern. There was also a spur that connected Horsted Keynes to Ardingly and Haywards Heath; this was opened on 3 September 1883. The

Southern Railway took the whole line over in 1923, although by this time the decline had set in. Like many rural lines the march of the motor car was taking its toll on passenger numbers and freight traffic alike

Under nationalisation British Railways took over in 1948 and by the early '50s closure plans were being drawn up. This wasn't a part of the Beeching grand plan for railway modernisation, that wouldn't be unveiled until 1963. Nonetheless, the line was closed by British Railways on 28 May 1955. However, following representations by a local resident, Miss Bessemer, it was discovered the closure was illegal due to an old act of parliament. Although ownership was passed through the Southern Railway to British Railways there remained a legal requirement to run a passenger service and so they were forced to run trains again. Unfortunately, however, for a second time the line closed on 16 March 1958 and another act of parliament was sought to sanction the closure legally.

In late 1959 a group of volunteers, keen not to see the line disappear into history, managed to lease the section of line from Sheffield Park to Horsted Keynes under a 5 year term. In 1960 the idea of a preserved railway was a new concept, people must have thought the idea mad. The keen bunch of volunteers really were pioneers of the railway preservation movement. The Bluebell (a nickname that stuck with the line due to the great display of flowers in springtime) provided a base for the rapidly disappearing steam locomotive, historical accuracy being at the forefront of what they where trying to achieve. I wonder if they could imagine or even hope that it would turn into the wonderful railway it is today and indeed that in the year 2013 it's still continuing to expand and grow.

The first trains ran for the newly formed "Bluebell Railway Ltd" in August 1960. The Bluebell Railway always had an eye on extension; however extending south from Sheffield Park would have been very difficult as a bridge had been removed. The spur from Horsted Keynes to Haywards Heath was also ruled out (certainly in the short to medium term) as a viaduct just West of Horsted Keynes had been demolished, so an extension north through West Hoathley to Kingscote and East Grinstead seemed the best option. In 1992 trains where running through Sharpthorne Tunnel (the longest tunnel on any heritage railway in the UK) for the first time and, the former station site at West Hoathley was operating as a temporary terminus (although passengers could not alight trains there). In 1994 trains began running to Kingscote, which had been purchased and renovated, including the rebuilding of the down platform and buildings. As previously mentioned, developments have continued in the years since and in March 2013 the extension to East Grinstead and reconnection to the national rail network was completed. Who knows what future developments are in store, maybe the spur from Horsted Keynes to Ardingly will be re-instated and that might even trigger a third book in the series!

If you haven't paid a visit to the railway, or maybe you haven't travelled on the extension through to East Grinstead hopefully this book will convince you that a visit is a must.

I'd like to thank all those who have helped make this book possible, from the volunteers who have created the railway we see today providing me with such a great photographic subject, to my family and friends who have helped me in putting the book together.

This is the Bluebell Railway Revisited. Take your seat and let the journey commence…

Matt Allen
Aldershot
April 2013

In this book you will take a journey along the Bluebell Railway from Sheffield Park to East Grinstead. These first few pictures will set the tone for what the railway has to offer. For me this is a classic Bluebell Railway image with P class number 178 resplendent in South Eastern and Chatham Railway livery hauling a mixed train.

Sussex at sunrise. On a cold December morning 53809 picks up the first rays of the morning's sunshine.

Opposite: In this photo 80151 has been dressed up as long lost classmate 80032,
which was built locally at Brighton works.

The Bluebell isn't just home to small locomotives: Bulleid Pacific number 34059 *Sir Archibald Sinclair* was fully restored at the Bluebell, returning to service in 2009.

Opposite: The Bluebell runs through some stunning Sussex scenery. Photographing scenes like this on a sunny morning is an absolute pleasure. 80151 is in charge of a Kingscote-bound service on a winter's day.

This book follows on from my original book on the Bluebell Railway published in 2008. This is the final image from that book where I suggested that the extension to East Grinstead was underway with the final planning permission being granted. Now in 2013, the destination board on Bulleid coach number 4279 is no longer wishful thinking … the extension of the line to East Grinstead in now complete.

The extension to East Grinstead has been a huge undertaking; raising the funds has been a big task. Luckily the support from enthusiasts, locals and visitors has helped bring the project to a successful conclusion.

It was a great thrill to be able to buy a return
ticket from East Grinstead for the first time!

There must have been a real feeling of pride for the staff when they were able to use this destination board for the first time.

BLUEBELL RAILWAY
WELCOME TO SHEFFIELD PARK STATION
OPENED BY THE L.B.& S.C. RLY.: 1st AUG. 1882
AS SHEFFIELD PARK AND FLETCHING
CLOSED BY BRITISH RAILWAYS: 13th JUNE 1955
(LAST TRAIN RAN ON 28th MAY)
OPENED BY BRITISH RAILWAYS
UNDER DURESS (THE SULKY SERVICE) 7th AUG. 1956
CLOSED BY BRITISH RAILWAYS: 16th MAR. 1958
OPENED BY BLUEBELL RLY.: 7th AUG. 1960
THE FIRST EX-BRITISH RLYS. LINE TO BE
PRESERVED BY ENTHUSIASTS

The railway hasn't forgotten its history and roots, as shown on this plaque
displayed at Sheffield Park Station. Sheffield Park Station is full of items
of interest if you go hunting.

Opposite: Let the journey commence. We'll travel north from Sheffield Park to
East Grinstead. Sheffield Park Station is now the southern terminus of the line. However
when the railway originally opened in 1882 the line ran further south to Lewes.

Sheffield Park is the headquarters of the railway, hosting the locomotive works, servicing depot and the carriage sheds. The footbridge in this photograph originally came from Lingfield Station.

A very Great Western scene deep in Southern territory! 9017 *Earl of Berkeley* (left) has been resident at the Bluebell since 15 February 1962 and was joined here for a special event by Great Western counterpart 3440 *City of Truro (right)* which is a part of the National Collection.

One of the recent developments at Sheffield Park has been the acquisition of the former Woodpax site. This has allowed for the carriage sheds in the left of this photograph to be built (under the name of Project Undercover). The provides some welcome undercover storage for the vintage rolling stock.

Opposite: With dark clouds gathering, Great Western Pannier Tank number 3650 waits to depart north from Sheffield Park.

The development of the Woodpax site has also allowed for a new museum to be built on platform 2. The museum has a magnificent array of interesting items – the new vibrant display areas show the items at their best. A visit to the museum is a must if you find yourself with spare time at Sheffield Park.

Opposite: During one of the railway's "War on the Line" events a number of Second World War vehicles are seen protecting Sheffield Park Station. The railway hosts a number of special events throughout the year; they certainly add even more interest for the visitor.

The station site has a great selection of period enamel signs. It is no surprise that the station has been used in many films and TV series including *The Railway Children* (1999 version) and more recently *Downton Abbey*.

Opposite: Bulleid Pacific 34028 *Eddystone* is seen on a cold evening at Sheffield Park.

The Bessemer Arms on platform 1 is a great place for a drink or bite to eat. The name of the pub comes from Miss Bessemer who blocked the original proposed closure of the line in 1955.

Opposite: 9F locomotive number 92240 was one of the last batch of locomotives to be built at Crewe Works being outshopped on 4 October 1958. It is currently stored at the Bluebell awaiting overhaul.

This is the crest on the side of H class locomotive number 263 which was photographed whilst at Sheffield Park. The SE&CR was formed on 1 January 1899, when the SER and LC&DR merged – hence the "Incorporated by Act of 1899" text. The SE&CR went on to become a part of the Southern Railway in 1923.

Shown on the nameplate of GB Railfreight locomotive 66739 is the Bluebell Railway crest, "Floreat Vapor" translates to "Let it Flourish". I can't think of anything that sums up the Bluebell Railway better.

Just north of Sheffield Park Station is Poleay Bridge. Here 34059 *Sir Archibald Sinclair*
is seen crossing the bridge heading towards Horsted Keynes complete with 'Golden Arrow' regalia
and a mixed train of British Railways Mk1 and Pullman coaches.

Heading southbound towards Poleay Bridge is long-time Bluebell resident E4 class locomotive number 32473. The late evening sunshine and the dark skies create a lovely scene.

Heading further north is a duck pond. I'd been after this photograph for some time, the only disappointment
was the fact the pond had sprung a bit of a leak and wasn't as full of water as I'd have liked!
However P class locomotive number 178 still created a pleasing reflection.

Opposite: During one of the railway's special events 32473 is seen with a demonstration goods train.
The short platform in the background is the now closed 'Ketches Halt' approximately ½ mile north of Sheffield Park.

After passing through Ketches Halt the trains start the climb of Freshfield Bank with an uphill gradient of 1-75. In this area there is a large number of photographic locations, and sometimes the cows and sheep can also be persuaded to add interest. The locomotive is 3650 which visited the line for a short period in 2012.

The type of morning that photographers dream of, and is probably the best photograph I've ever taken.
On a cold frosty morning visiting 7F number 53809 emerges from the mist at the bottom of Freshfield Bank.
The cold, still conditions helped to create a fantastic steam and smoke trail.

Heading southbound towards Sheffield Park the E4 locomotive is silhouetted against the sky.

King Arthur class locomotive number 30777 *Sir Lamiel* is owned by the National Railway Museum and is based at the Great Central Railway when not running on the mainline network. During a visit to the Bluebell Railway it was paired with Bulleid coaching stock, creating an authentic Southern Region train.

Another frosty and still sunrise on Freshfield Bank. Following on from the earlier photograph of 53809 getting similar conditions again was incredible. The locomotive is Terrier A1X *Stepney* albeit running as 32655 in British Railways livery.

Opposite: Seen further up Freshfield Bank H class number 263 hauls a great rake of vintage coaches. Of particular interest is the London and South Western liveried coach number 1520 at the rear of the train. Built in 1910 for use on the mainline out of Waterloo, the coach was restored in 2010 by the local carriage and wagon group based at Horsted Keynes, exactly 100 years after being built.

Sun and snow is the holy grail for railway photographers, mainly because it happens so rarely. This sequence of three photographs was taken on a December morning when the "Santa Specials" were running. In this photograph 80151 is caught climbing Freshfield Bank.

Getting around the roads surrounding the railway on this day was a little tricky, but well worth the effort. 34059 *Sir Archibald Sinclair* was another locomotive on "Santa Special" duties.

Taken in the same position as the previous photograph but in very contrasting conditions is 9F 92212. The loco visited the railway in 2012 and again at the time of writing in April 2013. It is normally based at the Mid Hants Railway.

Opposite: Maunsell U class locomotive number 1638 was the third loco in service on this snowy day. It was a testament to the railway that they actually managed to run any trains at all given the conditions.

80151 is a BR standard class 4MT (mixed traffic) locomotive. This class of locomotive totalled 155 and they could be seen all over the British Railways network. 80151 was built and Brighton in 1956 and arrived at the Bluebell in 1998.

Opposite: A truly vintage scene with Victorian coaches and an Edwardian locomotive.
The P class locomotive is seen climbing Freshfield Bank with two four-wheel coaches of London, Brighton and South Coast Railway and London, Chatham and Dover Railway heritage.

On a very hot spring day, evident by the lack of steam effect from the locomotive, 1638 heads a demonstration goods train.

Opposite: In this photograph 55 *Stepney* has been converted to British Railways livery using some clever vinyl overlays, although the lovely early morning light makes this less obvious. 55 is paired with a recently over-hauled South Eastern and Chatham Railway "Birdcage" coach. Note the extended guard's lookout at the end of the coach nearest the locomotive.

80151 is seen heading south towards Sheffield Park. This area is known locally as "Broken Bridge" due to the removal of an occupation bridge. You can just see the supports for the bridge adjacent to the rear of the train.

E4 class locomotive number 473 in Maunsell livery with matching Maunsell coaches is seen approaching Broken Bridge with the spring flowers just appearing.

The Bluebell Railway has a bigger collection of vintage coaches than any other preserved railway. Many of them come from railway companies that ended up constituting the Southern Railway. In this case Maunsell coaches built in the 1930s are seen behind 1638.

Opposite: With the lovely autumn colours beginning to show, 34028 (running as 34100 *Appledore*) rounds the curve at the top of Freshfield Bank.

In the same location as the previous photograph, about a mile and a half from Sheffield Park, the lineside provides a different perspective as 1638 works northwards to Horsted Keynes.

30777 *Sir Lamiel* picks up the light nicely as it climbs up the 1-75 incline.

Bulleid Pacific *Blackmoor Vale* number 21C123 was built in 1946 and is seen here carrying Southern Railway livery. During a steam gala event a fruit van was marshalled between the locomotive and the coaches for added interest.

Opposite: 53809 creating a great smoke effect when employed on "Santa Special" duty. These Christmas specials have proved extremely popular whilst hopefully attracting some of the young visitors to become the railway's volunteers of the future.

South Eastern and Chatham-liveried O1 class locomotive number 65 makes
good progress with a Kingscote-bound service.

Opposite: On a frosty Sunday morning the Dukedog 9017 takes the Pullman dining train from
Sheffield Park to Horsted Keynes in preparation for a lunchtime service. Whilst a Dukedog on a
Pullman train isn't exactly authentic it does create a very pleasing photograph.

7F class locomotives spent most of their days on the Somerset and Dorset Railway which sadly fell victim to the Beeching closures. 53809 is one of two 7Fs which were saved for preservation. It's seen here on a visit to the Bluebell with a demonstration engineer's train.

Opposite: "Chatham Twins", C class locomotive number 592 and O1 class number 65 both in South Eastern and Chatham Railway livery double head a rake of Metropolitan Railway coaches approaching Broken Bridge.

Passing through the site of the former occupation bridge is 30777 *Sir Lamiel*.

92212 was built at Swindon Works in 1959 and is the same class of locomotive as the famous *Evening Star*. These 2-10-0 locomotives were mainly built for heavy goods trains but did see occasional passenger use. Here the locomotive on loan from the Mid Hants Railway is seen at the top of Freshfield Bank.

A lovely spring scene with 80032 (actually 80151 in disguise) heading south towards Sheffield Park. Note the coach set number "862" on the end of the leading Bulleid coach.

Opposite: An interesting combination with two P class locomotives 178 and 323 bunker to bunker heading a mix of vintage coaches. The locomotives are in contrasting liveries, 178 *(leading)* in South Eastern and Chatham Railway livery whilst 323 is in "Bluebell" blue livery (the loco is actually called *Bluebell*).

A rather nice visiting combination was Great Western autotank locomotive 1450 and matching Great Western autocoach. These trains were a common sight on Great Western branchlines and allowed the train to be driven from both ends without moving the locomotive. This train is heading south towards Sheffield Park.

It must have been magical for families to turn up for a trip on a "Santa Special" with deep snow on the ground. 80151 is seen at Monteswood Lane heading towards Sheffield Park. The snow sticking to the roof of the coaches indicates how cold temperatures were.

On a lovely spring day 473 is heading a classic Southern Railway branchline train.

Opposite: The crimson and cream coach at the front of the train is one of two which are quite often used to form a "Lounge Car Service" serving afternoon teas. This livery is early 1950s whilst the green livery of the second coach was introduced in the late 1950s. During the transition of liveries mixed colour trains as seen here would have been a common sight. The locomotive is 80151.

As mentioned earlier 323 is in Bluebell livery, carries the Bluebell Railway crest and is actually named *Bluebell*. It was originally painted in this livery on arrival at the railway in 1961 and was returned to this colour scheme when overhauled and returned to service in 2011.

Opposite: Also seen heading south at Monteswood Lane is P class 323 with the late evening sun illuminating the train.

Another one of the smaller members of the Bluebell fleet is number 672 *Fenchurch*. This Stroudley-designed A1 Terrier class locomotive was built way back in 1872 and is seen here with a mixed passenger and goods train.

During the extension to East Grinstead a number of diesel locomotives were hired for use on engineer's trains. History was made on 7 March 2009 when electro diesel locomotive 73136, one of those hired, hauled the first ever diesel passenger service on the Bluebell. However steam fans need not fear; this isn't going to become a regular feature but was a special service to raise funds for the extension of the line.

Now we move north to Rock Cutting, just over 2 miles north from Sheffield Park; during a photographers' special, early on a frosty spring morning, 178 heads a vintage goods train northbound.

Opposite: Furness Railway number 20 is the oldest standard gauge steam locomotive operating in the UK. Built in 1863 this locomotive visited the Bluebell Railway in 2010. Early on an August morning number 20 heads south toward Sheffield Park.

A further photograph of Furness Railway number 20 shows how little protection the locomotive crew have from the weather: luckily the sun was shining!

Opposite: 178 heads a vintage train towards Horsted Keynes.

Shortly after being returned to service following its restoration, 34059 *Archibald Sinclair* is seen at Holywell. 34059 was built at Brighton Works in April 1947 and was withdrawn from service with British Railways on 29 May 1966.

Opposite: Carrying the British Railways black livery, 32473 is seen passing under the occupation bridge at Holywell, heading a train southbound towards Sheffield Park.

This photograph illustrates the Southern malachite green livery carried by 21C123 *Blackmore Vale*. The Bulleid Pacific locomotive is in its original "air smoothed" condition. A large number of the Bulleid Pacifics were rebuilt under British Railways (as seen in the earlier photographs of 34059 *Sir Archibald Sinclair*) and the air-smoothed casing was removed.

The same location as the previous photograph but in very different conditions,
1638 is seen on the last "Santa Special" of the day.

80151 heads south from Horsted Keynes on a summer's evening

The final bridge before Horsted Keynes is called "Three Arch Bridge". Using one of the three arches to frame 32473, it is seen heading an engineer's train southbound.

With the Three Arch Bridge just visible in the background, 1638 will soon be applying the brakes as it heads towards Horsted Keynes Station.

Opposite: The same train as the previous photograph from the opposite side of the line approaching Three Arch Bridge. I wasn't in two places at once but benefiting from a photographers' special where you can stage multiple "runpasts" in the same location.

Catching the last of the afternoon sunshine, 53809 heads towards Horsted Keynes.

Opposite: Looking at the lengthy grass it must be the middle of summer as locomotive Met1 heads a rake of Metropolitan Railway coaches. This is the authentic Metropolitan Railway combination that was recently used on the London Underground to run a number of specials to mark London Underground's 150th Anniversary.

During one of the railway's special events the opportunity was seized to run the great Southern combination of visiting locomotive 30777 *Sir Lamiel* and resident 34059 *Sir Archibald Sinclair*.

Opposite: Compared to the "Super Power" of the previous photograph 178 and two four wheel coaches look positively tiny as they approach Horsted Keynes.

With black skies and early evening sunshine providing some very interesting light, 1638 hauls a lovely restored Southern Region goods train.

Opposite: As the last few photographs demonstrate, the fields on the approach to Horsted Keynes showcase some really pleasing light on the build up to sunset. You can photograph either side of the line, with the north side being ideal for silhouettes. The locomotive is 53809.

As shown on this sign, sited in the lane outside Horsted Keynes Station,
the village is 1 mile away. It is a lovely Sussex village and well worth exploring;
the parish church of St Giles is one of the highlights.

Opposite: Horsted Keynes Station is a real gem and has been restored to the 1920s Southern Railway period. During a special event a Scammell "Mechanical Horse" resplendent in British Railways colours is posed outside the station.

This plaque displayed on the station platform is from the
National Heritage Railway Awards and is well deserved.

Opposite: Despite being in a very rural location Horsted Keynes Station has the look
of a London suburban station with multiple platforms and underpasses to connect the platforms.
On a spring morning during a photographers' special, locomotives 1638 and 473 can be seen.

With both locomotives in Maunsell livery various locations around the station were used, members of staff were also called upon to add to the atmosphere of the photoshoot. Here 473 is facing south towards Sheffield Park whilst 1638 rolls into the station.

Opposite: With dark skies behind, 1638 works a demonstration goods train through the station. Note the number of tracks leading into the station. The station limits have also undergone major signalling upgrades in recent years.

The railway has a good selection of restored goods wagons, most of them being of London, Brighton and South Coast, Southern Railway and South Eastern and Chatham Railway heritage.

Opposite: During one of the railway's very popular War on the Line events, Horsted Keynes Station seems to be in very good hands.

The War on the Line events are well attended and worth a visit, with a great selection of military vehicles and re-enactors dressed in all sorts of different costumes.

Opposite: Sitting between platforms 4 and 5, 80151 awaits its next duty.

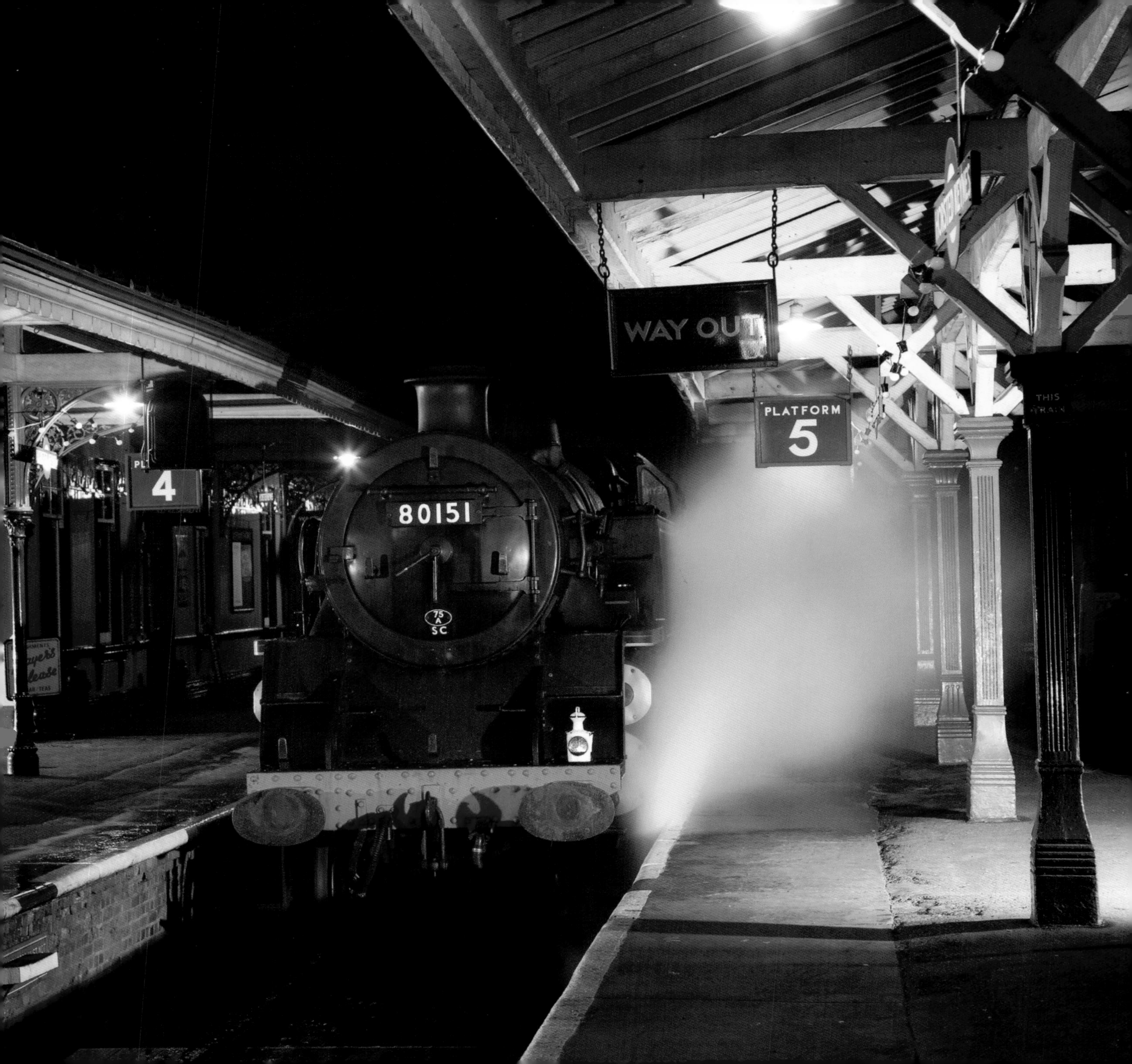

WAY OUT
PLATFORM
5
4
80151

A truly Southern scene; 80151 complete with Bulleid coaches.

Opposite: Rebuilt Bulleid Pacific number 34028 *Eddystone* visited the Bluebell from its base at the Swanage Railway. Here it is seen posing at Horsted Keynes.

During one of the railway's steam galas, two unrebuilt Bulleid Pacifics visited the line.
Here the two locomotives 34007 *Wadebridge* from the Mid Hants Railway and 34081
92 Squadron from the North Norfolk Railway are seen at Horsted Keynes.

Opposite: The railway's resident unrebuilt Bulleid Pacific 21C123 *Blackmore Vale*
is photographed recreating a Pullman boat train. The locomotive is in Southern Railway livery
which, when it became British Railways, was later renumbered 34023.

Just north of the station platform E4 number 473 is heading towards
the station with a goods train whilst 1638 awaits its next duty.

Opposite: In the final of the series of night scenes at Horsted Keynes an engineer's
train waits to depart north. The crew can be seen taking a welcome break.

VISIT THE CARRIAGE & WAGON WORKSHOP

← FILMS • DISPLAYS • INFORMATION

The Carriage and Wagon Workshop is based at Horsted Keynes where the railway's fine fleet of vintage coaches and wagons is restored. The restorations can vary from a repaint to complete rebuild from scrap yard condition.

Opposite: The Carriage and Wagon Workshop has a viewing area open to the public, accessed from platform 5. There is also a huge raft of information displayed about the projects undergoing restoration. A visit is strongly recommended.

This view is looking north and shows the platform layout at Horsted Keynes.
The driver of 473 can be seen oiling the locomotive.

E4 class locomotive 32473, seen here taking water, was built at Brighton Works in 1898 making it of Victorian heritage. The E4 class totalled 75 locomotives for use on the Southern and were used on both goods and passenger trains.

The wagon in this image is a SR 10 ton 5-plank open goods wagon. 900 of these were built in 1930/31 at the Southern Railway's workshops at Ashford, Kent. The station provides a great backdrop with the enamel signs adding to the 1920s look.

Opposite: Looking north, this photograph shows off the signalling at Horsted Keynes as 32473 rolls into platform 5.

The same engine as the previous photograph but in a different livery. In the days of the Southern Railway
the locomotive was number 473 (as seen here) becoming 32473 under British Railways.

Due to the angle of the sun, this photograph is only really possible in the middle of summer.
Furness number 20 approaches Horsted Keynes early on an August morning.

Taken from a village called Highbrook, looking down on a train heading north from Horsted Keynes towards Kingscote with the autumn colours in full glory. The locomotive is H class 263 on a lunchtime Pullman dining train.

Opposite: Nearly a mile north of Horsted Keynes Station is Horsted House Farm.
Here 32473 is passing under Horsted House Bridge heading south.

C Class locomotive number 592 heads a train of wooden vintage coaches north from Horsted Keynes. The coaches are a combination of four wheel coaches of London, Brighton and South Coast Railway and London, Chatham and Dover Railway at the front and Metropolitan Railway coaches at the back.

Just north of Horsted House Farm, 3650 heads towards Kingscote. 3650 is based at the Didcot Railway Centre and was steamed following a 20 year overhaul on 23 July 2008; the engine visited the Bluebell Railway in 2012.

With a length of 731 yards Sharpthorne Tunnel at West Hoathly is the longest tunnel on a preserved railway in the UK. This part of the line will be familiar to anyone who has watched the 1999 film version of the *Railway Children*. Here 1638 is on a goods train bound for Kingscote.

1638 makes a tremendous exhaust as it exits the tunnel and as can be seen in this photograph, trains are working uphill as this stage.   This was also the location for the original West Hoathly Station which was never rebuilt when the Bluebell Railway took over the line.

WHISTLE

N° 1638

32473 is seen exiting from the southern end of Sharpthorne Tunnel.

Opposite: 80151 (running as 80032) is seen near Birch Farm Crossing heading south from Kingscote. When this photograph was taken in April 2012 the locomotive was nearing the end of its 10 year boiler certificate and withdrawal from service.

Just over a mile south from Kingscote is Deans Crossing; here on a lovely spring
day 473 is heading south with a Sheffield Park-bound train.

Opposite: A driver's eye view!

With Kingscote Station just out of sight the charming Great Western autotrain heads south towards Horsted Keynes. Autotrains like this, formed of a Great Western 14xx class locomotives (here 1450) and an autocoach, would have been commonplace on Great Western branchlines.

The E4 473 is seen crossing Mill Place Bridge just south of Kingscote Station. Look how clear the lineside is of vegetation, not something you'll see on Network Rail these days!

With Kingscote Station in the background, 32473 heads south. The Bluebell reached Kingscote in 1994 and until the recent extension to East Grinstead it was the northern terminius of the line.

Opposite: 80151 (here running at 80017) is seen at Kingscote Station. After closure by British Railways the track was lifted in 1965 and the station sold as a private residence. Part of the station is still retained as a private house but it has been superbly restored to 1950s condition.

My original book, published in 2008, finished at Kingscote; just 5 years later and things have moved on. The objective of the Northern Extension Project, was to extend the line to East Grinstead. Whilst this is only a distance of 2 miles, as you'll see the size of the project was huge.

Opposite: Kingscote Station was built in 1882 by the London, Brighton and South Coast Railway, serving a few local houses with the closest village of Turners Hill about three miles away. 80151 (running as long lost classmate 80017) is photographed on a photographers' special.

Looking from the road bridge at Imberhorne Lane toward Kingscote in November 2012 you can see track laying progressing well. Negotiations with many landowners to purchase the track bed added to the scale of the project.

Standing on the same road bridge but looking towards East Grinstead shows the size of the problem! The cutting at Imberhorne had been used as a landfill site and had to be cleared, a huge undertaking. Most of the rubbish cleared from the site was removed by rail from the other end of the cutting.

On arrival at Horsted Keynes there was a naming ceremony, 66739 being named *Bluebell Railway*. It was particularly fitting that 66739 was chosen as this locomotive worked some of the engineering trains that helped clear Imberhorne Cutting.

Opposite: Taken from the same position as the previous photograph, what an amazing difference four months can make. Despite a very hard winter hampering work, history was made on 28 March 2013 when 66739 worked the first ever through train across the new extension of the line. This train ran from London Victoria to Horsted Keynes.

A few years ago I would never have thought I'd see a GB Railfreight class 66 at Horsted Keynes! The historic event of the first mainline train running across the new extension of the line attracted huge crowds.

Opposite: Steaming towards East Grinstead. During the first week of trains running to East Grinstead H class number 263 is seen from Imberhorne Lane halfway between Kingscote and East Grinstead.

The Bluebell Railway's new strapline is
"Now arriving at East Grinstead"…the wait is over.

Opposite: As well as clearing the cutting at Imberhorne another engineering task was the refurbishment of Imberhorne Viaduct. Unfortunately, the only shame with this impressive structure is the parapet walls are very high so photographing a train on the viaduct isn't really possible as a lot of the train is shielded from sight.

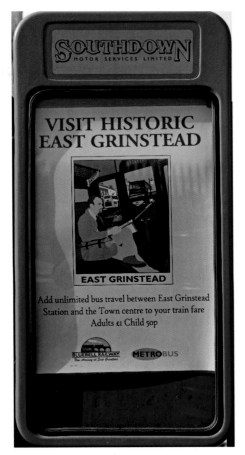

Despite limited space, period features add to the feel of East Grinstead Station.

Opposite: With no original station at East Grinstead a new platform has been built. The mainline station with direct trains to London Victoria is a few hundred metres away. Developments on the Bluebell site at East Grinstead continue with a signal box under construction.

The local press were very supportive of the opening of
the extension to East Grinstead.
(Reproduced with the kind permission of East Grinstead Courier and Observer).

Opposite: H class locomotive number 263 provides proof that steam has
made it to East Grinstead. Not only has the extension to East Grinstead
given the Bluebell Railway an extra 2 miles of track but it has now connected
the Bluebell Railway back up to the national network.

Looking from the new Bluebell Railway platform towards the mainline
East Grinstead Station, where an electric train can be seen in the platform

Opposite: 263 heads south from East Grinstead towards Sheffield Park. Imberhorne
Viaduct is just beyond the station limits and to the far right of this image you can just see
the track that connects the Bluebell Railway to the national network.

The new end of the line. What a huge achievement the Bluebell Railway has made by reaching East Grinstead. From negotiating with many landowners to purchase the trackbed, the construction of a new station site at East Grinstead, the refurbishment of Imberhorne Viaduct and to the clearing of Imberhorne Cutting, the completion of the extension is probably one of the biggest achievements in railway preservation. I hope you've enjoyed the journey.